THE UNDERGROUND RAILROAD

An Interactive History Adventure

Marcella. S

by Allison Lassieur

Mankato, Minnesota

You Choose Books are published by Capstone Press,
1710 Roe Crest Drive, North Mankato, Minnesota 56003.
www.capstonepub.com

Books published by Capstone Press are manufactured with paper containing at least 10 percent post-consumer waste.

Library of Congress Cataloging-in-Publication Data
Lassieur, Allison.
The Underground Railroad: an interactive history adventure / by Allison Lassieur.
p. cm.—(You choose books)
ISBN-13: 978-1-4296-0164-1 (hardcover)
ISBN-10: 1-4296-0164-7 (hardcover)
ISBN-13: 978-1-4296-1183-1 (softcover pbk.)
ISBN-10: 1-4296-1183-9 (softcover pbk.)
1. Underground railroad—Juvenile literature. 2. Fugitive slaves—United States—History—19th century—Juvenile literature. 3. Antislavery movements—United States—History—19th century—Juvenile literature. 4. Abolitionists—United States—History—19th century—Juvenile literature. 5. Slavery—United States—History—Juvenile literature. I. Title. II. Series.
E450.L34 2008
973.7'115—dc22 2007010509

Editorial Credits: Rebecca Glaser, editor; Juliette Peters, designer; Laura Manthe and Wanda Winch, photo researchers

Photo Credits: Corbis, 91, 94, 105; Corbis/Armstead and White, 64; Corbis/Bettmann, 6; Corbis/Edward Warren Day, cover; Corbis/Louie Psihoyos, 9; Cornell University Library/Division of Rare and Manuscript Collections, 20, 60; Hampton National Historic Site, National Park Service, 47, 48; Library of Congress, 15, 36, 42, 68; Library of Congress, Prints and Photographs Division, 16; Louisiana State Museum, 23; Maps.com, 11; Mendenhall Plantation/Rebecca G. Lasley, 79; North Wind Picture Archives, 25, 26, 39, 98; Ohio Department of Natural Resources, Parks and Recreation/Jim Glover, 29; Ohio Historic Preservation Office/Annie McDonald, 86; Ohio Historical Society, 30, 33, 35, 54, 74, 76, 102; Photographs and Prints Division, Schomburg Center for Research in Black Culture, The New York Public Library, Astor, Lenox and Tilden Foundations, 100; Salem Historical Society, 82; The Louisiana Collection, State Library of Louisiana, Baton Rouge, 12; The Virginia Historical Society, Richmond, VA (detail of painting Slave Auction), 57

Acknowledgement: Capstone Press thanks Paul Bernish at the National Underground Railroad Freedom Center in Cincinnati, Ohio, for reviewing this book.

Printed in the United States of America in North Mankato, Minnesota.
062012 006784R

Table of Contents

About Your Adventure

YOU are living in the 1850s, wrestling with the question of slavery. Will you break the law to help slaves gain their freedom?

In this book, you'll explore how the choices people made meant the difference between freedom and enslavement, between success and failure. The events you'll experience happened to real people.

Chapter One sets the scene. Then you choose which path to read. Follow the directions at the bottom of each page. The choices you make will change your outcome. After you finish one path, go back and read the others for new perspectives.

YOU CHOOSE the path you take through history.

Many slaves worked in cotton fields from dawn until dusk. They received no pay for their work.

CHAPTER 1

It's the 1850s, and the United States is less than 100 years old. Immigrants have come from all over the world to settle in America. The streets of New York and Philadelphia are filled with the rumble and clatter of carriages, wagons, and horses. Factories and businesses in the North provide jobs for newcomers.

In the South, life is quiet and slow. Farmland stretches as far as anyone can see. Cotton and sugarcane make plantation owners rich.

There's something else different about the South. In the South, there are slaves.

Turn the page.

Slaves live every day knowing they are someone else's property. The food they eat, the clothing they wear, and even their own families are owned by someone else. For most slaves, it is the only life they will ever know. But some slaves run away. They risk everything, even their lives, for freedom.

You've heard of abolitionists in the North who think blacks and whites are equal. Some of them lead runaways through unfamiliar areas or hide them from slave catchers. Their routes are secret. But their network is growing. It's become known as the Underground Railroad. And there's more need for it now than ever.

An abolitionist in Pennsylvania built these sliding shelves to hide runaway slaves in a crawl space.

Runaways used to be safe if they made it to the North. But since the Fugitive Slave Act of 1850 was passed, slave owners can recapture slaves in any state. The only place slaves can truly be free now is Canada. And the act makes it illegal to help slaves escape.

Turn the page.

As an American living in the 1850s, you're not sure how you feel about that. You understand how important it is for slave owners to reclaim their property. How else would Southern plantation owners make a living?

Another part of you is uneasy at the idea of owning another human being. What if the abolitionists are right and all people are equal? Then slavery, and everything the South stands for, would be wrong. There are so many sides to this question, and there are no easy answers.

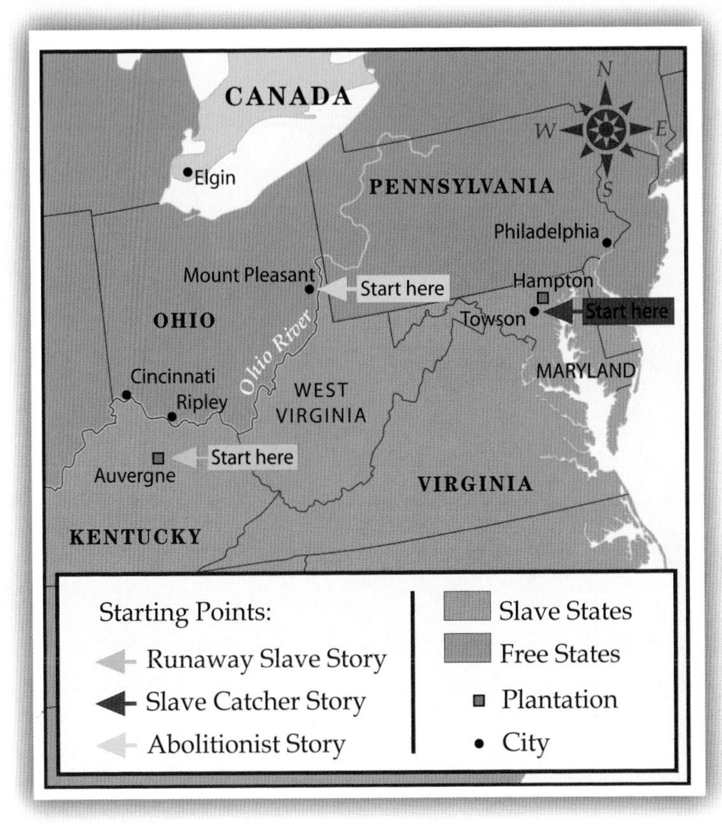

To experience what it's like to be a runaway slave, turn to page **13**.

If you want to see what it's like to be a slave catcher, turn to page **43**.

If you have the courage to break the law and be an abolitionist on the Underground Railroad, turn to page **75**.

Plantation owners had grand homes and large estates. Slaves worked in the gardens, the fields, and the big house.

CHAPTER 2

RUNNING TO FREEDOM

It's a beautiful spring morning in Kentucky. You're in one of the grand flower gardens that fill the yard around a large, beautiful home. The house is called Auvergne.

From the big house, you hear someone calling you. A knot of fear tightens in your stomach. You know that voice. It's the voice of your master, Brutus Clay. You are his slave.

You were born here. Your mother and father are also slaves. Your father works in the master's fields every day, from sunrise to sunset. Your mother works in the kitchen.

Turn the page.

"I want every flower bed weeded by sundown," Master Clay says to you. You have no choice, so you quickly get to work.

Hours later, your back aches and your hands are bleeding from pulling all the weeds. You glance back at the house as it grows dark. Through the window, you see Master Clay and his family sitting down to an elegant dinner.

You run toward the slave cabins. Black-eyed pea soup is bubbling in a pot over the fireplace. Your mother and father are talking frantically.

"Are you sure? How many of us will be sold?" your mother cries.

Sold? Your heart pounds and you can't breathe. Being sold away from your family is the worst thing imaginable.

Slaves lived in small cabins on their masters' plantations.

"I don't know how many," Father says. "But we can run before the slave trader comes."

"Run away? That's crazy talk! They'll hang us," your mother says.

"I have the money Master Clay let me keep when I worked on his neighbor's farm last fall," Father says. He stands up straight. "Better to die in freedom than live a slave. Come with me."

Turn the page.

Brutus Clay was the largest slaveholder in Kentucky.

Your mother refuses. Your baby brother is too little to travel, she says.

They come up with a plan. Master Clay is going to hire out Father to his neighbor again next week. Father will get a pass to travel to the other farm. That's when he'll escape. When he is free, he will earn enough money to buy the rest of the family.

Then they both look at you. "You're old enough to decide," Father says. "You can come with me. Or you can stay here with your mother."

What a terrible choice! If you go with your father, you risk being recaptured and sold. Or you could die in the wilderness. But you might make it to freedom. If you stay, you could help your mother. But you might be sold away from your family forever. What will you do?

If you choose to stay with your mother, turn to page **18.**

If you choose to flee with your father, turn to page **20.**

You can't leave your mother, no matter how sweet freedom sounds. Later that week, your father leaves. Three days pass before Master Clay realizes that your father isn't coming back. He sends for you and your mother.

"Where is he?" Master Clay demands.

"I don't know," your mother cries, shaking her head.

The next week, a slave trader comes to Auvergne. He speaks to Master Clay and hands him money. The slave trader chains your wrists.

"Come with me," he says roughly. You can hear your mother begging Master Clay not to sell you as you're thrown into the back of a wagon. The last thing you see is your poor mother collapsed in the dirt road, screaming and crying for you.

The stern man tells you he is the manager of a huge sugarcane plantation in Louisiana. For the rest of the trip, he makes you walk behind the wagon. At night, you have to sleep on the ground. It's cold, but the man doesn't give you a blanket.

Several days later, you arrive at the Mississippi River. You and several other slaves are chained together on the deck of a boat. Most of them don't talk much. Like you, they miss their families.

You lose track of the days. You and the rest of the slaves are forced to stay on the deck, no matter what the weather. Rain drenches you. The sun beats down, and there's no shade. Nights are cold. All you can do is sit on the deck with your head in your hands. The chains seem to grow heavier each hour.

Turn to page **22.**

The pull of freedom is strong. You decide to go with your father. You make a plan. When your father gets permission to leave, he will wait for you in the woods a few miles down the road. After dark, you will join him. Then you'll both head north, toward the border of Kentucky and the free state of Ohio.

Slave tags like this one were required for slaves who traveled between plantations.

Two days later, Father comes to the cabin. He shows you a small metal tag hanging around his neck. It's his pass to leave Auvergne. You're scared and excited at the same time.

The next afternoon, Father leaves as expected. The hours until dark seem to drag by. Finally, all the lights in the big house go off. You slip out the door and run, keeping to the shadows. Soon you see your father's tall figure.

You and your father walk all night. Suddenly, a black man on horseback rounds the bend in the road.

If you choose to ask this man for help, turn to page **24.**

If you choose to move on alone and risk your life in the wilderness, turn to page **28.**

When the horrible river journey ends, you're loaded on another wagon. A short time later, the wagon turns around a bend in the road. Spread out in front of you is the largest farm you've ever seen. Miles of fields stretch in every direction. A large building stands near the fields. The huge sugar processing machines inside are rumbling and clattering. Overseers with their whips yell at groups of slaves to work harder.

The manager pulls you out of the wagon, and your legs collapse from fear and hunger. He hauls you up as a large man approaches.

"Here's the overseer of Ashland," the manager says to you. "Do what he says." He turns to the overseer. "Here's a new one for the fields."

Slaves likely helped build the great house at Ashland Plantation in Louisiana. It was completed in 1842.

The overseer takes the chains off and hands you over to another slave. "Get this one some food," he barks. He looks at you. "You'll start in the fields in the morning."

Turn to page **26**.

At first your heart thumps with fear. Then your father says, "I know him." Father speaks to the man. He shows the man his pass.

"He says he'll take us somewhere safe where we can rest," Father says. The man takes you through the woods to an isolated cabin. Your father tells him about the plan to escape to the North. You can only think of food and sleep.

When you get to the cabin, you open the door and tiredly stumble inside. Your father and the man are right behind you. The man slams the door and locks it behind you. Then he grabs you and pulls out a gun. It's a trap!

The man claps you both in chains, then throws you and Father in the back of a wagon. The man laughs. "You know the punishment for running away?" he sneers. "Master Clay could order up to 100 lashes with the whip!"

Slave catchers often set traps to catch runaway slaves.

Hope dies inside you. You could be whipped, too. You might even be hanged, as an example to other slaves of what happens when someone tries to escape. All you can do is hope that Master Clay will be kind to you when you return.

THE END

To follow another path, turn to page 11.
To read the conclusion, turn to page 101.

Even children had to work in the sugarcane fields. Overseers made sure slaves got the job done.

Two weeks have passed. Each morning, you go into the sugarcane fields with hundreds of other slaves. Your job is to hoe dirt over the sugarcane stalks after they are planted. You learned on the very first day that the dirt over the newly planted stalks must be exactly 3 inches deep.

The overseer saw you hoeing less dirt. He pulled out his whip and gave you five lashes. When you got up, the blood made your clothes stick to your skin. But you didn't dare stop or cry. You picked up your hoe and ran to catch up with the others. The blood dried on your back and made your clothes stiff and sticky.

At sundown, you walk to the cabin you share with several other slaves. There is no furniture. Every night as you fall asleep on the hard wood planks, you wonder what happened to your family. Did Father escape? Was Mother sold? You will probably never know. And they will likely never find out what happened to you. You have little chance of escape now.

To follow another path, turn to page 11.
To read the conclusion, turn to page 101.

"Do you trust him?" you ask your father.

"No," Father says. "Let's keep going." Father shows the man his pass. The man eyes it suspiciously and then rides away. You know he could be a slave catcher.

You and Father dash into the woods. It's well past daylight when you feel safe enough to stop. You drink from a small brook and then fall asleep under some bushes.

All day you rest in the woods. By evening, you feel stronger. You wait until the stars come out, and then Father points to the sky.

"See that group of stars that looks like a cup with a handle?" he asks. You nod. "It's called the Drinking Gourd. It points to the North Star—and to freedom."

Runaway slaves followed the Drinking Gourd, now called the Big Dipper, and the North Star to find their way.

Turn the page.

For days, you wander through the woods. There's always the danger of wild animals or a slave owner's dogs finding you. You're hungry all the time.

One night you reach the bank of a wide river. There's a bright light across the river. You just make out a house on top of a hill.

The village of Ripley, and freedom for runaway slaves, lay across the Ohio River.

"That land across the river is Ohio," Father says. "Freedom!" You can't believe that you're looking at a free state.

Along the shore you see a figure dressed in dark clothing and carrying a lantern. You and your father duck behind a large bush so you won't be seen.

As you look at the wide, cold river, your heart sinks. "How are we going to get across?" you whisper miserably.

Father stares at the river, and then looks at the man. "Looks like we have two choices," Father says finally. "Swim across, or ask that man for help."

If you choose to try to swim across the river, turn to page **34**.

If you choose to ask the man for help, turn to page **32**.

Slowly, you and your father approach the man, who's standing near a boat. To your surprise, you see that he's black.

"Welcome, friend," the man says. "We heard that there were two runaways in the woods nearby." He shakes Father's hand. "I'm John Parker. I'm a conductor on the Underground Railroad. My friend is waiting for us in the village of Ripley, on the other side of the river."

You all climb into the boat. On the other side, a white man helps you out.

"This is the Reverend John Rankin," Mr. Parker says. On a big hill in front of you is the house you saw from across the river. You climb 100 steps to the house.

The steps to John Rankin's house were climbed by many escaped slaves.

Go to page **35.**

"We have to swim across," Father says finally. "The water is cold, but we can do it!"

You're afraid of the big river, but you're more afraid of getting caught. You both quietly wade into the water. It's freezing! The current is very strong, but you're a strong swimmer. So is Father. You're so close to freedom!

As soon as you start swimming, you realize this was a big mistake. The river is much wider and stronger than you thought. You're too weak from hunger, fear, and weeks of travel to keep swimming. You feel yourself being dragged down. The last sight you see is your father's head bobbing in the water. You join the many slaves who died on their way to freedom.

To follow another path, turn to page 11.
To read the conclusion, turn to page 101.

A white woman with a kind face welcomes you. "Come in," she says, "I'm Jean Rankin." Soon you and Father are eating warm stew and fresh bread. No food has ever tasted better.

"My house has been the door to freedom for many human beings," Reverend Rankin says. "Tonight you can sleep in safety."

You curl up under a blanket beside the fire and fall asleep peacefully.

Reverend John Rankin helped more than 3,000 slaves escape while living in Ripley, Ohio.

Turn the page.

John Rankin's house stood on the highest point of a hill overlooking the Ohio River.

The next day, Reverend Rankin and Father discuss where you should go. "It's not safe for you to stay here," Reverend Rankin says.

"Isn't Ohio a free state?" you ask.

"Yes, but the Fugitive Slave Act lets slave catchers come into free states and recapture runaway slaves," Reverend Rankin explains.

"Then what should we do?" you ask.

"You could go to Cincinnati. It's a huge city with a large black population. Many former slaves live and work there. Or you could go to Canada. Slavery is illegal in the whole country. Your father can buy land and own his own farm in Canada."

Father's eyes light up at the idea. "I would love to have my own farm," he says. "But I also need to get a job now so I can make enough money to buy my wife and baby. I miss them so!"

"Mr. Parker and I will help you, no matter what you choose," Reverend Rankin replies.

If you choose to go to Cincinnati, turn to page **38**.

If you choose to travel on to Canada, turn to page **40**.

Cincinnati is about 50 miles away. That night, you go to Mr. Parker's house. You and Father get into a wagon, and Mr. Parker hides you among boxes.

Mr. Parker takes you to a small church, where several black people are there to meet you. Mr. Parker tells you that this is a black church. The church members help the Underground Railroad. A kind black woman gives you and Father food and a warm bed. The next night, another church member takes you to Cincinnati.

When you reach Cincinnati, you're taken to the home of Samuel and Sally Wilson. They give you a safe place to stay for the night. "We know many people who can help you," the Wilsons assure you.

Cincinnati was a destination for many runaway slaves.

Abolitionists in Cincinnati help Father find a job and a place to live. Here, you hope to blend in with the huge black population of the city. You try to breathe easier. Maybe you're free at last.

To follow another path, turn to page 11.
To read the conclusion, turn to page 101.

You realize that in Canada, you will never fear being recaptured. Reverend Rankin and Mr. Parker arrange for you and Father to take a train to Canada.

After a long train ride, you reach Toronto. There, you meet several free blacks who tell you about a settlement called Elgin. It is a community made up mainly of runaway slaves. At Elgin, your father buys a small farm with the money Reverend Rankin gave him. Soon he's planting his own crops. You go to school for the first time in your life. Even more amazing, some of your classmates are white!

For the first time in the weeks since you left Auvergne, you feel truly free. If you and Father work hard and save money, someday you can buy your mother and little brother. You'll bring them to Canada, the place that former slaves call "The Promised Land."

To follow another path, turn to page 11.
To read the conclusion, turn to page 101.

$100 REWARD!

RANAWAY

From the undersigned, living on Current River, about twelve miles above Doniphan, in Ripley County, Mo., on 2nd of March, 1860, A NEGRO MAN, about 30 years old, weighs about 160 pounds; high forehead, with a scar on it; had on brown pants and coat very much worn, and an old black wool hat; shoes size No. 11.

The above reward will be given to any person who may apprehend this said negro out of the State; and fifty dollars if apprehended in this State outside of Ripley county, or $25 if taken in Ripley county.

APOS TUCKER.

Slave owners offered rewards for the return of their slaves.

CHAPTER 3

SLAVE CATCHER: ON THE HUNT

All your life you've lived on a small farm near the town of Towson, Maryland. Your family has always been poor. A few months back, a local plantation owner asked if you would find one of his runaway slaves. He couldn't spare his overseer to look for the runaway. You found the runaway hiding in the woods, and the owner gave you a reward. You realized that you could make a lot of money catching slaves.

Turn the page.

One day, you read notices in the newspaper about runaway slaves. One of them catches your eye. It's from Mr. Ridgely, who owns a nearby plantation called Hampton. Maybe he would hire you.

That same day, you see a notice tacked up at the store. The notice offers a $50 reward for the capture of a young black woman named Mary. She's run away from a plantation in Virginia.

You could look for either one of these runaways. There's a reward for the return of the girl. But sometimes plantation owners offer extras, like payment for expenses. You stand to make a nice profit either way. Which slave do you decide to try to find?

If you go visit Mr. Ridgely at Hampton, turn to page **47.**

If you set out to find the girl, go to page **45.**

You think that finding the girl won't be too much trouble. The notice says that she was recently sold to a nearby farmer.

You search the area for several days. Finally, you spot a camp in the woods. That night, you hide and wait. Sure enough, after dark a short young woman appears. You step out of your hiding place, pistol drawn.

"Mary?" you ask with a grin. "I've been looking for you."

Mary's face falls. Tears well up in her eyes. "Don't shoot me, sir," she pleads. "I'll come with no fuss. My mistress will give you a reward for me."

Turn the page.

The sign said the reward was $50. That's more than you make as a farmer in a year. But you know that some slaves are worth far more than that at auction. Especially young female slaves like Mary. You could return her to her owner, knowing that you'd get the reward. Or you could gamble that you'll make more if you sell her yourself.

*To return Mary for the reward money, turn to page **50**.*

*To sell her yourself, turn to page **56**.*

Hampton was owned by several generations of the Ridgely family.

When you arrive at Hampton, you're shown into a huge room filled with expensive furniture.

"I hear you have a runaway slave," you say to Mr. Ridgely when he comes in.

"Yes. Henry Jones. He's one of my favorites," Mr. Ridgely replies. He describes Henry as 5 feet, 9 inches tall, light skinned, with full lips and a lean face.

Turn the page.

John Ridgely owned Hampton in the mid-1800s. He had about 60 slaves, including Henry Jones.

"When did he go missing?" you ask.

"A few weeks ago."

You frown. You know that the longer a slave has been gone, the less likely he'll be found. But you're determined to try. "I can find him for you," you say.

"If you find him within the county, I'll pay you $50. If you find him outside the county, I'll double it," Mr. Ridgely says. He also agrees to pay your expenses, which you tell him are 6 cents a mile and $2 a day. You shake hands on the deal.

Now, where do you look? Henry has been gone so long, he's probably not anywhere nearby. Maybe someone local saw Henry before he left. Pennsylvania is the nearest free state. You've heard of the Underground Railroad helping runaways make it to Philadelphia.

If you decide to ask around town, turn to page **51.**

If you go to Philadelphia, turn to page **67.**

"Come on," you say gruffly. You tie Mary's hands and lead her back to your house. The next day, you put her in the back of your wagon and start out for her owner's farm. The trip will take at least a week, but you don't mind. You know that there will be a reward for you.

You and Mary travel every day. At night you stop and make camp. You chain Mary to the wagon so she won't escape. The third night out, you're awakened by a noise. Slowly, you draw your pistol and peer into the dark woods beyond your camp. You hear a slight rustling noise. It could be a deer. Or it could be something else.

If you choose to investigate the noise, turn to page **60**.

If you choose to roll over and go back to sleep, turn to page **53**.

No one around town has seen a slave that matches Henry's description. You decide to ask the local patrollers. If anyone knows about runaways in the area, it would be them.

Patrols are groups of men who ride everywhere, looking for slaves. You thought about joining a patrol, but decided against it. Patrollers don't get paid, and you wanted to make some money.

The storekeeper is one of the patrollers. "We caught a male slave a few days ago. Arrested him for stealing a chicken," the storekeeper says. His description of the man doesn't quite match Mr. Ridgely's description. It could be Henry, though.

"What happened to the slave?" you ask the storekeeper.

Turn the page.

"We threw him in the county jail," the man replies. "He's probably still there."

"No," a man in the store pipes up. "He escaped before the patrol could get him into the jail. I hear he's hiding out in the woods a few miles from here."

"I'm sure they put him in the jail," the storekeeper insists. "I saw him there myself."

Great. Now what do you do?

If you choose to go to the jail, turn to page **54**.

If you choose to search the woods, turn to page **59**.

The next morning you awake. Mary is gone! The chain on the wagon is still there. The lock on the metal cuff is broken. Cursing, you look everywhere. But you know that Mary is long gone. She could have gone in any direction. You decide not to go after her.

Reluctantly, you turn your wagon around and start home. On the way, you wonder if Mr. Ridgely still needs someone to find his runaway slave Henry. Cheered by the thought, you start to whistle. Slave catchers always have work, and you're sure to find more.

THE END

To follow another path, turn to page 11.
To read the conclusion, turn to page 101.

Once Harriet Tubman escaped slavery, she risked her life to free other slaves.

At the jail, the sheriff confirms that the patrol brought in a slave last week.

"Can I see him, please?" you ask. "I'm looking for one of Mr. Ridgley's runaways."

"He escaped two days ago," the sheriff says.

"Did you look for him?" you ask.

"Why should I?" the sheriff says. "He ain't getting far around here. Either the patrol will catch him, or he'll starve to death in the woods."

"Either that," the sheriff continues, "or he was helped by that Harriet Tubman."

You've heard of Harriet Tubman. She's a former slave. Now she works as a conductor on the Underground Railroad. Rumor says that she travels between Maryland and Philadelphia, helping runaways to freedom. If Harriet Tubman helped Henry, he's as good as gone. But you're not willing to give up yet.

Going to the jail was a waste of time. Or was it? If the escaped prisoner was Henry, you know he's only had a two day head start. If it wasn't, you may be on a big wild goose chase.

If you decide to check the woods for Henry, turn to page **59.**

If you think Henry escaped north and you decide to head to Philadelphia, turn to page **67.**

The trip to Mary's plantation will take too long, you think. It could be days, maybe weeks, before you get the reward. It's better if you sell her yourself.

Two days later, a crowd gathers at the auction house. One by one, each slave is brought onto a stage. The buyers poke and prod them. They pinch the slaves to see how strong their muscles are. The white men put grubby hands into the slaves' mouths, inspecting their teeth. They make the slaves run, march, and jump up and down.

When Mary is brought up, the auctioneer says, "This is Mary. She's low in stature but well-proportioned, of strong and healthy appearance, and of dark copper color."

Slaves went to the highest bidder at auctions.

The bidding gets lively, with three men competing to buy her. When the gavel comes down, Mary is sold for $200. As she is led away, you're given $100, your share of the sale.

Turn the page.

The auctioneer approaches you. "She was a fine specimen," the man says. "If you get any more like her, bring them here. I'll make sure they sell for a good price."

You smile. You'll be back. There will always be other slaves.

THE END

To follow another path, turn to page 11.
To read the conclusion, turn to page 101.

The next day, you ride all over the county, through the woods where slaves might be hiding. Near a road, you see a black figure crouching behind a tree.

"What are you doing there?" you ask.

"I'm running an errand for my master . . . um, Mr. Stanley," the boy says. His voice is shaking.

You know Mr. Stanley. "He doesn't own any youngsters," you reply.

"He just bought me last week," the boy says.

"Okay, then, show me your pass." You know that slaves must have a pass to travel off the plantation.

"I lost it," the boy says. He starts to cry.

If you choose to let the boy go, turn to page **62**.

If you choose to take the boy prisoner, turn to page **64**.

Slowly, you get up and sneak into the woods. It must be a deer, you think. Then you hear a thin cough.

"Stop!" you shout, pointing your pistol at the noise. "I'll shoot! Identify yourself!"

"Don't hurt me," a voice says. It's Mary.

You grab her arm and drag her back to camp. You examine the chain that held her to the wagon. The lock on the metal cuff is broken.

Chains were used to keep slaves from running away while they were being transported.

Grumbling, you fish two chains and cuffs out of the back of your wagon. You put one on Mary's wrist. The other one goes on Mary's ankle. Then you attach them both to the wagon in such a way that Mary is forced to stand up all night.

"Maybe this will teach you not to run," you say gruffly. Tears roll down Mary's cheeks. You ignore them. "And no food for you tomorrow." You know that a hungry and exhausted slave is less likely to try to escape.

Turn to page **63.**

You're pretty sure the boy is lying. But you don't have time to deal with him. Besides, he's a kid. He could be telling the truth. And if he's running away, he won't get far.

"Get out of here, boy," you say gruffly. "If I ever see you out alone again I'll whip you myself."

"Yes, yes!" the boy shouts as he runs down the road. "Thank you, thank you."

As you watch him, you think that you could have sold him yourself and made some money. But Henry is the bigger prize. Tomorrow you'll head for Philadelphia. Maybe you'll have better luck there.

Turn to page **67.**

You don't have any more trouble. Three days later, you arrive at the plantation.

As you drive up, a little girl yells, "Mama, Mama!" Mary jumps out of the wagon, and the girl grabs her neck, hugging her tightly.

"My baby, my baby!" Mary weeps. "I didn't think I'd ever see you again."

A white woman appears. "Did you find my Mary?" she asks. "I'm so glad! I was having such a time training Ruth to clean the floors just so!"

The woman turns to Mary. "How dare you put us in such a bind, you worthless girl," she scolds. "And only a week before our big party! How could you be so uncaring?" Mary bows her head and says nothing.

Turn to page **66**.

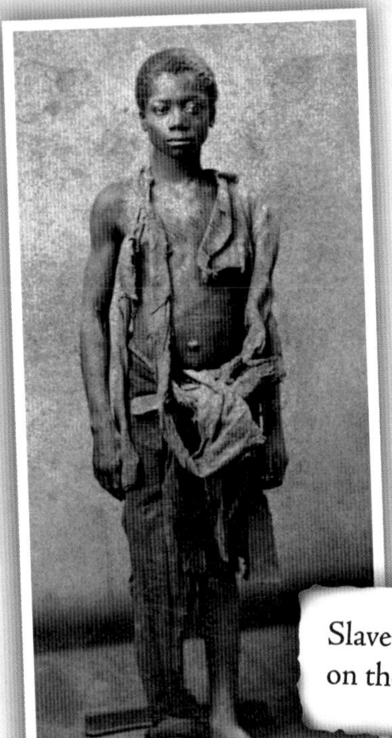

Slaves had little but the clothes on their back when they escaped.

"Well, we'll see about that," you say. You clap the boy in chains and take him to the jail.

"I found this one in the woods outside of town while I was looking for Henry Jones," you say. "Says Josiah Stanley is his master."

"Stanley don't own no kids," the sheriff says. "Boy, where are you really from?"

Crying, he admits that he's from a plantation in Virginia. He got lost trying to find his mother, who was sold a few weeks ago.

The sheriff puts the boy in a jail cell. He writes a letter to the boy's owner in Virginia. If the owner comes for the boy, the sheriff will get the reward money. If not, he can sell the boy.

As you leave the jail, the sheriff stops you. "I heard talk of a group of abolitionists from Philadelphia who come down here to help runaway slaves. That Henry you're looking for might be in their company."

"Thank you," you say. "I had thought to try Philadelphia next."

Turn to page **67**.

You clear your throat. "Um, ma'am, I'm here for the reward," you say.

"Of course!" the woman replies. She pulls out a small purse. "There's $50 in gold coins. Thank you so much for bringing back my Mary." Then she takes Mary roughly by the arm into the house.

You get into your wagon and head for home. This reward will buy food and clothing for your family for several months. And there will always be other slaves to find.

To follow another path, turn to page 11.
To read the conclusion, turn to page 101.

It's dangerous being a slave catcher in Philadelphia. The Fugitive Slave Act makes it legal for you to go there and recapture runaway slaves. But many abolitionists in the city help runaway slaves. And they hate slave catchers. You'll have to be careful.

When you arrive, you spend days watching known Underground Railroad stations like the Johnson House. You hire a black informant to spy on William Still. You know he hides runaway slaves at his home on South Street.

Turn the page.

William Still helped escaped slaves who came to Philadelphia.

One day, your informant tells you he saw a black man who looks like Henry at Still's home. You start watching his house yourself. Sure enough, one night a tall black man leaves the house with several other men. He looks like Henry, but you're not sure.

It's too dangerous for you to confront them alone. A mob of abolitionists would likely tear you apart! But that black man really looked like Henry. You could follow the men to see where they go. Or, you could take the safe route by returning to Maryland and telling Mr. Ridgely that his slave is lost.

If you follow the men, turn to page **70.**

If you return to Maryland, turn to page **72.**

It's dark, so the men don't notice you following them. They go into a building downtown. This must be where William Still's abolitionist group meets. You watch the building.

An hour later, the black man comes out—alone! You can't believe your luck. You walk across the street.

"Henry Jones?" you ask politely.

The man turns. In a flash, you realize it's not Henry after all. But maybe you can capture this one and sell him. You quickly pull out a set of shackles and try to slap them on the man's wrists.

"Help!" he yells. "A slave catcher!"

The door bursts open, and men pour into the street. Suddenly you're surrounded.

Panicked, you push through the crowd and race down the street. The mob roars behind you, but you don't dare look back. You dash through alleys, hiding in the maze of streets. The sound behind you dies down, and you stop, gasping for breath.

You lost them.

You're lucky to have escaped. You limp back to your carriage and head out of town. Mr. Ridgely might be angry you couldn't find Henry, but there's nothing more you can do.

Turn the page.

You go back to Maryland and tell Mr. Ridgely your story. "I'm disappointed," Mr. Ridgely says. "Henry was one of my most trusted boys. I just don't understand why he'd leave such a good life here. But it sounds like he's not coming back."

"Thank you for your work," he continues, paying you for your expenses.

"You know, sir," you say, "If you had hired me sooner, I might have been able to find Henry before he got too far."

"You're right," Mr. Ridgely replies. "I shouldn't have waited so long to hire you. I thought Henry would come back in a few days. They usually do. Next time I'll contact you straight away."

You nod. You know that there will be plenty of work from Mr. Ridgely and other slave owners in the area.

THE END

To follow another path, turn to page 11.
To read the conclusion, turn to page 101.

The Free Labor Store in Mount Pleasant, Ohio, refused to sell goods made by slave labor.

CHAPTER 4

THE ABOLITIONISTS' STORY

You've always believed slavery is wrong, but not everyone agrees with you. You belong to the Society of Friends, also called Quakers. This religious group thinks slavery is wrong. But some Quakers think it's wrong to break the law to help slaves. You are not one of them.

You decide to move to an area where you can help runaway slaves. You buy a farm outside the small town of Mount Pleasant, Ohio. Many townspeople there are against slavery. There's even a Free Labor Store that will not sell anything made by slave labor.

Turn the page.

David Updegraff was part of the Underground Railroad in Mount Pleasant.

One day you meet a gentleman named David Updegraff. You've heard that Updegraff is very active in the Underground Railroad. Some people say that he's helped dozens of runaway slaves.

"Good morning, friend," he says pleasantly. "Are you settling in?"

"Yes, I feel at home here," you reply.

"I'm glad to be among people who have the same anti-slavery feelings I do."

"Good, good," Updegraff says. Then he pauses. "As you well know, many of us here in Mount Pleasant are part of the Underground Railroad," he says gravely.

"How can I help?" you ask.

"Thank you for your offer," Updegraff replies. "We need conductors who can take slaves to other stations on the Underground Railroad. We also need a stationmaster who could house and feed slaves when they pass through town. Which one would you like to do?"

If you choose to become a conductor, turn to page **78.**

If you choose to become a stationmaster, turn to page **81.**

"Excellent!" Mr. Updegraff says. "We'll be in touch when we have slaves who need transport."

Three days later, you receive a strange note. It says, "I have three horses for sale: a stallion, a mare, and a foal. If interested, please visit my barn tomorrow night. If you do not want these horses, I will ask Mr. Daniel Hise of Salem if he is willing to take them." The note is signed "D. Updegraff."

The note is in code! But you figure out what it means. Three slaves are on their way. You are to meet Mr. Updegraff at his farm tomorrow night and take them to Mr. Hise, the next stop on the railroad.

When you arrive, Mr. Updegraff takes you to the barn. There, huddled in the shadows, are three slaves: a father, mother, and their 6-year-old son. They look at you with fear and hope.

Wagons with hidden compartments were used to secretly transport escaped slaves.

"You're safe now," you say. You and Mr. Updegraff show them a secret compartment in your wagon. They crawl into it and you carefully close the door. You pile hay on top to hide the compartment.

Turn the page.

At last, everything is ready for you to leave. You're excited and afraid. If a slave catcher finds you, you could be arrested.

The first few hours go by quickly. Then, as you round a bend, you see a man standing in the road. He signals at you to stop. You've never seen this man before. You get uneasy. Is this a trap?

If you stop and talk to the man, turn to page **82**.

If you choose to drive on, turn to page **90**.

You put a lighted lantern in the window every night so runaways know your home is a safe house. A few nights later, you get a knock on the door, very late. It's Updegraff. He leads two young black men wearing tattered clothing into your house. Their names are John and David. They're exhausted and terrified. But they also have the light of freedom in their eyes.

"You're free now," you say. "Have some food and be comfortable."

After they eat, you give them each a new set of clothes. "Now I feel really free," John says. "These are my first clothes as a free man."

You lead them to the barn, where they will sleep for the night. Just as you are starting to fall asleep, you hear another knock. At the door is a black man you've never seen before.

Turn to page **84**.

Daniel Hise lived in Salem, Ohio, north of Mount Pleasant.

You slow the wagon to a stop.

"Are you Mr. Updegraff's friend? The one who is buying the horses?" the man asks.

"Why do you want to know?" you reply.

"I am Daniel Hise," the man says. "I am anxious to have the horses in my possession. I have heard there are horse thieves out tonight!"

Slave catchers! You nod and motion for Hise to get into the wagon. "They are safe in the back," you whisper.

"Good, we must hurry," Hise says. You drive your horses as fast as they can go, hoping that you make it to Hise's farm before daybreak.

No such luck. Just a short way down the road, a gang of slave catchers with guns blocks the way.

"Stop!" one of them shouts. "Stop now, I say!"

If you decide to stop and let them search the wagon, turn to page **85**.

If you decide to turn around and try to run, turn to page **91**.

"Please, sir, let me in," the man begs. "I've got slave catchers on my tail!"

You are immediately suspicious. Sometimes slave catchers set traps like this to catch people helping runaways. But if this man is a runaway, he'll be in danger if you turn him away. What do you do?

If you choose to open the door, turn to page **88**.

If you choose to tell the man to go away, turn to page **94**.

Your heart thumps as you slow the wagon to a stop. The slave catchers swarm the wagon. "I know you, Hise," one slave catcher says. "Are you hiding runaways?"

"No, sir," Hise says smoothly. "I've been on my friend's farm, helping with chores."

"This time of night?" one slave catcher sneers. Any minute, you think, they'll find the secret compartment.

"Of course not," Hise replies. "We worked until dark and my friend kindly gave me food and a bed. But I've got my own chores, so I need to get back early."

Turn the page.

You hold your breath. Amazingly, they seem to believe Hise's story. The leader motions to the men, who move away from the wagon. You sigh in relief. You and Hise watch as the gang rides away. As soon as they're out of earshot, you tap on the floor of the wagon.

"Are you all right?" you ask softly. You hear a light tap in reply.

Daniel Hise's house in Salem, Ohio, had secret rooms under the house where he could hide runaways.

You race to Hise's farm. Then you help the runaways out of the wagon and into the house.

"I have a secret room where you can stay for a few days," Hise says to the fugitives. "When you're rested, we'll get you to the next safe house further north."

You stay and rest, too. You'll return to your farm tomorrow, ready to help the next group of runaway slaves.

To follow another path, turn to page 11.
To read the conclusion, turn to page 101.

You can't turn the man away. But just as you open the door, several white men with guns appear out of the darkness. It's a trap!

The men push their way into your home. Shouting, they destroy everything in your house. The furniture is thrown into the yard and set on fire. Your clothing is tossed into the trees. All your food is thrown into the dirt.

"Where are they?" one man yells, pointing a rifle at your head. When you don't answer, he pushes the gun into your ear and says, "If you turn them over to us, we won't kill you."

You're terrified. But you continue to insist that you are not hiding slaves. The gang searches the rest of the house and the barn, but find nothing. The runaways must have heard the commotion and gotten away, you think with much relief.

The slave catchers finally leave, but everything in your house is destroyed. Strangely, as you look at the damage, you're not angry. Instead, this attack makes you more determined than ever to fight slavery.

THE END

To follow another path, turn to page 11.
To read the conclusion, turn to page 101.

The only safe thing you can think of is to drive past the stranger. As you do, he yells at you to stop. "I'm waiting for someone who is looking to buy some horses," the man says. "Would that be you?"

"Perhaps," you reply nervously. "Who are you and why do you want to know?"

"I'm Daniel Hise," the man says. "Updegraff told me to find you," he says. "He got word that there are horse thieves on the roads tonight. It's not safe to complete the transaction now."

You hesitate. How do you know this isn't a trap? "You must trust me," he says. "Either turn around and go back, or follow me into the woods."

If you choose to turn around and go home, turn to page **97**.

If you decide to follow Hise, turn to page **98**.

Slave catchers attack a wagon of escaped slaves.

You feel the panic rise in your chest. Now that they've seen you, your only chance is to run, you think. You turn the wagon around as quickly as you can.

You push the horses as fast as they can go. The slave catchers give chase, yelling "Stop!" and shooting their guns in the air. Your heavy wagon will never outrun them, so you finally stop.

Turn the page.

The slave catchers swarm onto the wagon. It's not long before they find the secret compartment.

"So, what's this?" the leader asks, jabbing the runaways with the butt of his rifle. The men grab you and Hise and throw you in the back of your wagon along with the three runaways. The slave catchers tie you up and drive back to Mount Pleasant. Soon you find yourself in a bare jail cell with Hise. You've been arrested under the Fugitive Slave Act.

The day of your trial comes. The courtroom is packed with friends, family, and neighbors from Mount Pleasant. The evidence is presented. The trial is short, because you admit to helping the runaways.

"Guilty!" the judge says and he sentences you to 30 days in jail and a $500 fine. You are quickly hustled away to the jail.

You know the time will pass. It's a small price to pay for helping slaves escape. You hear that the family was broken up and all three—even the little boy—were sold away. The news makes you even more determined to continue your work once you get out of jail.

THE END

To follow another path, turn to page 11.
To read the conclusion, turn to page 101.

Slaves' clothing was often tattered and torn by the time they arrived in the North.

You tell the man to go away. He begs you again—the slave catchers are right behind him! If they find the others in the barn, you'll all be killed. Quickly, you think of a plan. You put on the man's threadbare coat and hat. Then you send him to the barn to warn the others.

You run to the road and start walking slowly. Soon a gang of slave catchers appears.

"Stop!" they yell. "Who are you? Why are you here so late at night?"

"I'm passing through," you say casually. "I'm on my way to Salem, and I'm anxious to get home."

The men look at your shabby clothing and laugh. But one stares at you. "So you've been on the road for hours?"

"Yes," you reply.

"Then you must have seen a runaway slave who came by here a little while ago."

"Why yes, I did see a black man a few miles back," you say, thinking quickly. "Said he was free, though. He was going to Cincinnati to find work."

Turn the page.

After a few more questions, they seem satisfied and leave. When you're sure they've gone, you run home. The runaways are still huddled in the barn with the man, terrified.

"It's no longer safe for you here," you say. "The slave catchers are gone, but they might come back."

The next morning you send a coded message to Updegraff. "I cannot take the horses you offered," you write. "There are too many horse thieves in town these days."

At dawn the next day, Updegraff arrives with a wagon and takes the runaways to the next station on the Underground Railroad.

To follow another path, turn to page 11.
To read the conclusion, turn to page 101.

"I'll go back home," you tell Hise. "I'll keep the horses in my barn tonight," you say.

"Good," Hise says. "Make sure they stay out of sight. I'll contact you when it's safe."

You drive home slowly, so as to not arouse suspicion. Thankfully, you don't see anyone on the road. For the next week, you live in fear that the runaways will be discovered.

A few days later, you receive word from Hise that it's safe to try again. That night you load the family into the wagon and make your way to Hise's farm. This time, you arrive safely. Even though this adventure is over, you know there will be another one soon.

THE END

To follow another path, turn to page 11.
To read the conclusion, turn to page 101.

Swampy, wooded areas were good hiding places for slaves trying to escape.

When you get safely into the woods, you and Hise open the secret compartment. The runaways look terrified.

The woman lays a trembling hand on your sleeve. "Thank you," she says softly. "Thank you for saving us tonight."

For the first time, the importance of what you're doing hits you. These are not just runaways. They're people, with hopes, dreams, and fears just like yours.

You unhitch the horses. Quickly you put the runaways on horseback and plunge deeper into the woods. Hours later, near dawn, you arrive at a small shack near the edge of a swampy area. You and Hise help the exhausted runaways bed down for a few hours of sleep.

You realize that it might be too dangerous for you to go back to your house. You decide to stay here until the slave catchers have left and then return home.

To follow another path, turn to page 11.
To read the conclusion, turn to page 101.

Harriet Tubman is pictured on the left, with several of the former slaves she helped bring to freedom.

CHAPTER 5

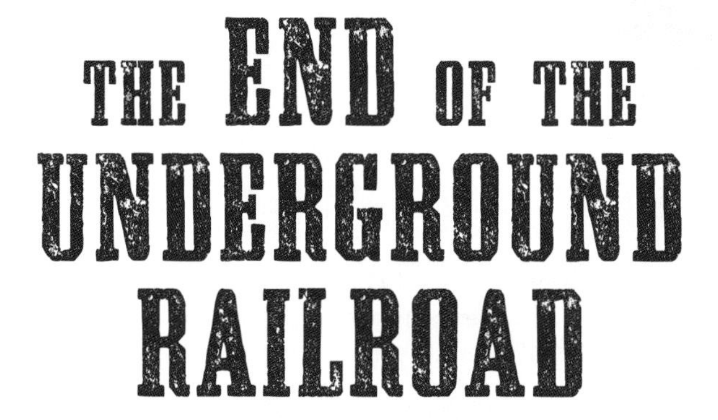

THE END OF THE UNDERGROUND RAILROAD

The Underground Railroad helped an estimated 70,000 to 100,000 slaves escape between the 1830s and the start of the Civil War in 1861. Every year more people joined the Underground Railroad to work as spies, informants, stationmasters, and conductors.

Conductors such as Harriet Tubman, a former slave, sneaked into slave states to guide runaways to freedom. In some cases, slaves on farms and plantations worked as conductors. They put themselves in great danger to help their fellow slaves escape.

Stationmasters, such as John and Jean Rankin, housed slaves in their homes. Often whole families supported Underground Railroad efforts. Levi and Catherine Coffin always had their home in Newport, Indiana, ready for escaped slaves who might come there.

Levi Coffin gave escaped slaves a place to rest in his Indiana home.

Slave owners and Southern politicians didn't sit back and let all this happen. Slaves were a big investment for their owners. Cotton and sugar were the basis of the Southern economy. Without slavery, the huge plantations couldn't function. To plantation owners, slavery was necessary. Politicians passed local and state laws to control slavery and keep the slaves from running. Slave catchers roamed everywhere, looking for fugitives.

Tension over slavery kept growing. In Congress, senators from Northern states fought and argued with Southern senators. Southerners were convinced they had the right to govern themselves as they wanted. If they wanted to keep slaves, they insisted, it was no one's business. Northerners didn't agree.

In 1860, Northerner Abraham Lincoln was elected president. Southern states saw his election as a defeat for themselves and their desires for self-government. Beginning with South Carolina, 11 states seceded from the Union. They formed their own nation, the Confederate States of America. Lincoln said that these states had no right to secede. This disagreement led to the Civil War.

The start of the Civil War led even more slaves to try to escape. In 1863, President Lincoln signed the Emancipation Proclamation, which freed all slaves living in states that had seceded. Slaves fled the South by the tens of thousands. Many former slaves became soldiers for the Union. By the end of the war, slavery had all but ended. In 1865, the 13th Amendment to the Constitution ended slavery for good.

This group of freed slaves worked with the 13th Massachusetts Infantry Regiment during the Civil War.

The need for the Underground Railroad was gone. The abolitionists who had worked so hard to end slavery now focused their efforts on helping newly freed slaves.

At a huge rally in Cincinnati, Levi Coffin announced the end of the Underground Railroad. He said, "Our underground work is done, and as we have no more use for the road, I would suggest that the rails be taken up and disposed of."

Time Line

1793—The first Fugitive Slave Act is passed, stating that slaves must be returned to their owners.

1822—Reverend John Rankin moves to Ripley, Ohio, and begins helping slaves escape.

1835–1850—Slave Henry Jones appears in records at Hampton.

1845—Brutus Clay of Bourbon County, Kentucky, reports owning 57 slaves.

1849—John Parker moves to Ripley, Ohio.

1850—The Fugitive Slave Act of 1850 allows slaveholders to retrieve slaves in Northern states and free territories, and makes it illegal to help runaway slaves.

1850—An advertisement for runaway slave Henry Jones appears in the local newspaper. Henry Jones never returns to Hampton.

1850–1860—Harriet Tubman makes 19 trips into Maryland to free about 300 slaves.

1860—Abraham Lincoln is elected president of the United States. South Carolina secedes from the Union.

1861—The Civil War begins after Confederate forces fire on Fort Sumter.

1863—Abraham Lincoln signs the Emancipation Proclamation, which frees slaves in the Confederate states. Many freed slaves fight for the North in the Civil War.

1865—The Civil War ends and the 13th Amendment to the U.S. Constitution outlaws slavery.

1870—The 15th Amendment gives African American men the right to vote.

Other Paths to Explore

In this book, you've seen how events surrounding the Underground Railroad look different from three points of view.

Perspectives on history are as varied as the people who lived it. You can explore other paths on your own to learn more about what happened. Seeing history from many points of view is an important part of understanding it.

Here are some ideas for other Underground Railroad points of view to explore:

- Plantation owners in the 1800s depended on slaves to get their farm work done. What was it like to own slaves?

- Besides helping fugitive slaves, abolitionists published articles and gave speeches to convince others that slavery was wrong. What was it like to try to change something that many people favored?

- Abraham Lincoln was not in favor of abolishing slavery at the beginning of the Civil War. What things happened to change his mind?

Read More

Landau, Elaine. *Fleeing to Freedom on the Underground Railroad.* Minneapolis: Twenty-First Century Books, 2006.

Lemke, Donald B. *The Brave Escape of Ellen and William Craft.* Mankato, Minn.: Capstone Press, 2006.

Rossi, Ann. *Freedom Struggle: The Anti-Slavery Movement, 1830–1865.* Washington, D.C.: National Geographic, 2005.

Stearns, Dan. *Harriet Tubman and the Underground Railroad.* Milwaukee: World Almanac Library, 2006.

Internet Sites

FactHound offers a safe, fun way to find Internet sites related to this book. All of the sites on FactHound have been researched by our staff.

Here's how:

1. Visit *www.facthound.com*
2. Choose your grade level.
3. Type in this book ID **1429601647** for age-appropriate sites. You may also browse subjects by clicking on letters, or by clicking on pictures and words.
4. Click on the **Fetch It** button.

FactHound will fetch the best sites for you!

GLOSSARY

abolitionist (ab-uh-LISH-uh-nist)—a person who worked to end slavery before the Civil War

auction (AWK-shuhn)—a sale where goods are sold to the person who bids the most money

conductor (kuhn-DUK-tur)—a person who helped runaway slaves escape to the North on the Underground Railroad

fugitive (FYOO-juh-tiv)—someone who is running from the law

informant (in-FOR-muhnt)—someone who gives information, often to help catch someone else

overseer (OH-vur-see-uhr)—a person who watches over and punishes slaves, to make them work harder

patrol (puh-TROHL)—a group of volunteers who kept watch for runaway slaves

plantation (plan-TAY-shuhn)—a large farm where crops such as cotton and sugarcane are grown; before 1865, plantations were run by slave labor.

station (STAY-shuhn)—a hiding place such as a house, cellar, barn, or church on the Underground Railroad where slaves could rest and be safe

Bibliography

Blassingame, John W., ed. *Slave Testimony: Two Centuries of Letters, Speeches, Interviews, and Autobiographies.* Baton Rouge, La.: Louisiana State University Press, 1977.

Blight, David W., ed. *Passages to Freedom: The Underground Railroad in History and Memory.* Washington, D.C.: Smithsonian Books, 2004.

Bordewich, Fergus M. *Bound for Canaan: The Underground Railroad and the War for the Soul of America.* New York: Amistad, 2005.

Campbell, Stanley W. *The Slave Catchers: Enforcement of the Fugitive Slave Law, 1850–1860.* Chapel Hill, N.C.: University of North Carolina Press, 1970.

Documenting the American South: Slave Narratives http://docSouth.unc.edu/neh

Franklin, John Hope, and Schweninger, Loren. *Runaway Slaves: Rebels on the Plantation.* New York: Oxford University Press, 1999.

Siebert, Wilbur. *The Underground Railroad from Slavery to Freedom.* New York: Russell & Russell, 1967.

Still, William. *The Underground Railroad: A Record of Facts, Authentic Narratives, &c.* Chicago: Johnson Publishing Company, 1970.

Index